THE PSYCHOLOGICAL NATURE OF BULLYING AND ITS DETERMINANTS

THE PSYCHOLOGICAL NATURE OF BULLYING AND ITS DETERMINANTS

A Study of Teenagers Living in the Country of Georgia

Nato Asatiani

**THE PSYCHOLOGICAL NATURE OF BULLYING AND ITS DETERMINANTS
A STUDY OF TEENAGERS LIVING IN THE COUNTRY OF GEORGIA**

iUniverse books may be ordered through booksellers or by contacting:

iUniverse
1663 Liberty Drive
Bloomington, IN 47403
www.iuniverse.com
844-349-9409

Because of the dynamic nature of the internet, any web addresses or links contained in this book may have changed since publication and may no longer be valid. The views expressed in this work are solely those of the author and do not necessarily reflect the views of the publisher, and the publisher hereby disclaims any responsibility for them.

Any people depicted in stock imagery provided by Getty Images are models, and such images are being used for illustrative purposes only.
Certain stock imagery © Getty Images.

ISBN: 978-1-6632-5813-7 (sc)
ISBN: 978-1-6632-5784-0 (e)

Library of Congress Control Number: 2023922236

Print information available on the last page.

iUniverse rev. date: 01/22/2024

CONTENTS

PREFACE

Adolescent bullying and violence is a very common occurrence and is regarded as one of the most acute problems in the world. Bullying has sparked much attention in recent years, and neither the public nor the media stay indifferent to such cases. Bullying manifests itself with particular ferocity in school settings. Bullying is a multicomponent and multifaceted social phenomenon, making its identification, prevention, and management rather difficult. Hence, it is crucial that experts and the public are informed about the phenomenon of bullying. To this end, the public should have access to scientific studies on bullying as well as reliable information sources based on these studies about the nature of bullying, its forms, and the peculiarities of its manifestation.

The actual empirical study, which models the psychological mechanism of bullying and identifies the predictors leading to the execution of the said behavior in the example of teenagers in Georgia, is an extremely interesting part of this book. According to the study, a positive, trustworthy school culture hinders the development of bullying behavior. It is substantiated with high statistical reliability that regardless of the background (mean) aggression, the quality of school culture can be decisive in the implementation or prevention of bullying behavior.

This study provides a clear picture of the current situation in Georgia regarding bullying and school culture. The descriptive study results outline the types of school cultures and victimization trends according to factors including region, school size, student gender, age, and parental occupation. The results are extremely interesting both for the analysis of the situation and for the initiation of further and more in-depth and large-scale descriptive studies. Finally, the work concludes with presenting the study findings and practical recommendations for teachers, parents, and educators.

ABSTRACT

The goal of our research was to study the phenomenon of bullying within the school culture and, in combination with the factors that trigger aggression, to construct a psychological model of its operation mechanism. To this end, we studied recent literature available in the field and decided to base our research on the anthropic theory of set that stems from the Georgian school of psychology. According to this theory, the basis for any psychological activity or action is an internal psychological mechanism—the set—that emerges as a result of interaction of three components: presence of demand, presence of an object that can satisfy the demand, and presence of instrumental possibilities (conditions) that make the satisfaction possible. We assumed that such dispositional sets formed the psychological mechanism for bullying. That is, if the school culture did not allow the realization of aggression, the victimization would not occur, despite the presence of vulnerable risk groups. Hence, we assumed that despite the level of aggression, schools that maintained a safe and secure culture would have lower levels of victimization, but the schools with an unsafe culture would display high levels of victimization.

To test our hypothesis, we applied three questionnaires. We studied levels of aggression using the Buss-Durkey Inventory; to study the school environment, we applied a questionnaire by A. Bochaver and associates that focuses on the emotional atmosphere in the classroom and school. We also used a questionnaire by H. Mynard and S. Joseph to assess levels of victimization.

In all, 1,422 students from ninth through twelfth grades took part in the survey. We constructed a hierarchical regressive model, which allowed us to conclude that the basic variables of our model, in fact, explain 34 percent of victimization. Particularly, it was revealed that the variables of the educational environment and the levels of aggression in classrooms—or rather, their combination—account for 73.02 percent of the total (34 percent) influence revealed through regression.

The most powerful factor that influences the scale of victimization is a combined variable of aggression and the type of the school culture, the threat. Our survey demonstrated that the probability of turning into a victim (victimhood) is highest among those teenagers who sense threats in their school environments. However, in a school culture based on maintaining communication rules and mutual respect, therefore providing a sense of well-being to the students, the probability of the teenager becoming a victim is lower.

Overall, our survey results showed that the negative school environment, in combination with aggression, is a predictor enhancing the practice of bullying. A safe school environment is a predictor lessening victimization.

Concurrently, the survey also revealed predictors not connected with the school culture. They include parental employment and the size of the school. With these variables, on the later stages of our survey, we assessed types of school cultures and levels of victimization. We then studied the differences between their means. The differences of means between these variables revealed a remarkably interesting picture, particularly in terms of parental employment. When neither parent worked, or only the mother worked, a small but statistically significant predictor of victimization was identified. The comparison between school sizes yielded interesting results as well. Students felt most comfortable in schools with a student population that ranged between three hundred and eight hundred.

We believe the recommendations that stem from these and other findings of our survey will benefit the planning of secondary education policy in Georgia.

INTRODUCTION

Bullying has become a growing problem worldwide. We encounter cases of bullying everywhere: at school, in the streets, as well as in the environment where young people tend to get together. Hence, it is critical to explore the psychological nature of bullying as one of the key challenges of the twenty-first century and to analyze the cases that impel teenagers to engage in such behaviors.

Bullying is considered a subcategory of aggressive behavior. However, it implies psychological rather than physical harm, and unlike standard aggressive behavior, it tends to have a repetitive nature, and its permanent nature exacerbates its consequences. Consequently, bullying always has a purposeful and repetitive nature.

The forms of bullying and the factors influencing it are the subjects of many studies. We found an interesting observation: In parallel with physical and verbal bullying, researchers focused their attention on the form of social bullying that distinguishes it from any other aggressive behavior. It is demonstrated by exclusion of the teenager from the group, which, in most cases, becomes more difficult for the teenager to overcome than any other type of aggressive behavior.

Looking at the statistics, we can assume that it is difficult to find a student who has not been a victim of bullying, a bully himself/herself, or has been involved in bullying in some form at least once. While studying the essence of bullying, researchers often highlight the roles of the family, peers, and school, which suggests that the environment plays a distinctive role in terms of preventing bullying. Numerous studies show that culture, community, traditions, and values can deeply impact the development of a teenager, as well as the frequency of occurrences of aggressive behavior in those particular cultures and communities.

Scientists talk a lot about the psychological peculiarities of a victim, a bully, and assistants (supporters or accomplices), which we also discuss in detail in terms of our work. In all mentioned three cases, the focus is made on the environment, which, on the one hand, can turn an aggressive teenager into a bully, and, on the other, can become a predictor for a teenager to be turned into a victim.

Consequently, since we saw that the environment contributes a lot to both bullying and its prevention, we decided to explore the issue at the school culture level and assume that in the case of a safe school culture, bullying would be less likely to occur than in an unsafe school environment. In this regard, we analyzed the international experience of different school administrations. As the analysis demonstrated, teenagers felt more protected in a school environment where values and principles are not imposed on the students, which resulted in less bullying.

The studies, conducted at various times, also show that bullying not only violates a student's physical or emotional safety but also has a negative impact on the entire learning/teaching process. Teenagers engaged in bullying, especially the victims, tend to have low academic achievements and low levels of involvement in school life. Consequently, analysis shows that the presence of bullying in schools hinders the realization of one of the main principles of education—the provision of holistic development for students. Today, everyone agrees that the goal of education is no longer only transmission of knowledge. It also implies the development of a teenager as a free person with universal values.

In terms of desk research, we have clearly observed that bullying has been studied and analyzed from many scientific angles. Studies have described the cases of bullying from various aspects, as well as different conditions and factors for its implementation. True, bullying is interestingly explained by multiple psychological theories, but it is obvious that how it is displayed requires additional analysis and study.

That is why we decided to study the psychological nature of bullying and its determinants in a sample of students in Georgian secondary schools. Since it is based on the general psychological theory of behavior and mental activity, we decided to develop a psychological model of a bullying action.

It should be also noted that if we judge various aspects of bullying based on the analysis of scientific studies available on the issue, we will clearly identify three main factors that affect bullying. These factors are: personal aggression, the presence of the object (victim) on which to carry out the aggression, and the environment or the conditions available in the environment. Hence, we can assume that for bullying to occur, the presence of aggression (demand), victim (object of demand), and environment (instrumental conditions) is required. The interaction of these three factors is well explained by the theory of set. And because of that, we decided to study the psychological nature and mechanism of action of bullying using that theory.

In compliance with our beliefs, the psychological mechanism of bullying lies in dispositional sets, the instrumental possibilities of which are embedded in the classroom climate. Therefore, the main hypothesis of our study is:

> The kind of the school environment at the background of aggression is a key determinant of bullying behavior, and when school culture does not allow the realization of aggression, even though there are always vulnerable risk groups in the classroom, they cannot be victimized.

To test this hypothesis, we conducted an empirical study of the degree of aggression, school climate, and victimization among the students.

MAIN RESEARCH HYPOTHESIS
AND METHODS

As mentioned previously, analysis of the studies conducted on bullying and available scientific literature showed that it is necessary to explore not only individual causes of bullying, but also to develop a psychological model of the origin and realization of this behavior. Therefore, the goal of our survey is to study the psychological nature of bullying and its determinants on the example of Georgian secondary-school students. And in addition, to construct a psychological model of bullying action based on the general psychological theory of behavior and mental activity set.

We assume that the bullying behavior emerges in the case when three major components overlap. These components are personal aggression, the object required to realize aggression, and a conducive environment for acting out the aggression. In our opinion, it is the unity of these three factors that makes the realization of bullying behavior possible.

Hence, the goal of our survey is to show that there must be aggression, the object of aggression (victim), and the environment that will enable the bully to display the aggression. Consequently, we think that bullying should be understood as the result of a unity (system) of factors, not just the behavior influenced by particular factors.

We have already mentioned that the theory of set helps us to better understand this model, according to which, in order to implement the behavior, it is necessary to develop a set that is created by: (A) demand, (B) the object satisfying the demand (victim), and (C) instrumental possibilities (environmental factors).

In compliance with our considerations, the psychological mechanism of bullying lies in dispositional sets, the instrumental conditions of which are embedded in the classroom climate. Thus, the main hypothesis of our research is:

> The kind of the school environment at the background of aggression is a key determinant of bullying behavior. If the school culture does not allow realization of aggression, then even though there are always vulnerable risk groups in the classroom, they cannot be victimized.

We are making an assumption that bullying can occur in the presence of aggression, a potential victim, and favorable conditions for such a behavior.

Hence, the main hypothesis of our study can be formulated as two subhypotheses:

1. Regardless of the level of aggression, a safe school environment significantly reduces the cases of bullying. More precisely, we can state that regardless of the level of student aggression,

a safe school environment predetermines a low level of victimization.

2. Regardless of the level of aggression, an unsafe school environment predetermines a high level of victimization.

Concurrently, we can assume,

3. The cases of bullying occur more often among boys than among girls.

Proceeding from the fact that it is easier to establish positive school culture in small schools, we assume that

4. The smaller the size of the school, the fewer the cases of bullying.

And finally, we also assumed that parental unemployment would be an important independent variable for the study of the psychological mechanism of bullying, as it negatively affects the students' social status and psychoemotional state, as well as the age and region of the students where they live. At the same time, assessing the impact of these variables would provide us with additional information that will be interesting for general education policy planning.

To test our hypotheses, we used three questionnaires for the survey and examined the level of aggression, the forms and frequency of victimization among teenagers, and the school environment.

1. *Aggression Level Survey:* We used a Buss-Durkey Inventory[1] to identify forms of aggression among teenagers. The

---

[1] Buss-Durkey Inventory, 1957.

questionnaire is designed in English and contains seventy-five test items and comprises eight scales. In the study, we used the version of Buss-Durkey Inventory that was tested and adapted by Amiran Grigolava and Bella Arutinova at the Institute of Psychology. The questionnaire consists of the following forms of aggression display: physical aggression, indirect aggression, irritability, negativity, resentment, jealousy, verbal aggression, sense of guilt.

2. *School Environment Survey:* In order to study the school climate, we used the questionnaire[2] developed by Bochaver and associates in 2014. the goal of which is to study the emotional background in the classroom and at school. The questionnaire contains forty-six questions grouped into four blocks. These blocks are: "threat" (sixteen questions), "wellness" (eleven questions), "isolation" (ten questions), and "equality" (nine questions).[3] Students' levels of *threat* are assessed according to how teenagers respond to the questions, by means of which it is found whether interference, abusive action, making fun of somebody that makes the whole class laugh, giving offensive names, and so on are acceptable at school. In terms of the questionnaire, students also evaluate their classes. They have to answer the question of whether their classes are evaluated as a hooligan class and so on. To assess the sense of *wellness*, students should explain whether they can leave their belongings in the classroom freely and even more so, in the corridor; whether it is a common

---

[2] Alexandra Bochaver, 2014.

[3] We used the version of the test adapted by Elene Chomakhidze and Mari Kikalishvili in 2018.

experience to go on excursions with teachers; whether their teachers enjoy being their class master, and so on. The *isolation* scale measures fights among students and their attitudes toward such behavior. Particularly, how acceptable fights are and whether they occur frequently. Also, when they happen, are they considered as an exception, leading to long-lasting discussions, and so on. And finally, the information on the *equality* scale is accumulated by using the following statements: If there is a fight, do you discuss it for a long time? During the breaks, we enter other classrooms, our class has the reputation of being a good class, and so on.

Hence, the dimensions of an unsafe school environment are the scales of threat and isolation that, according to our hypothesis, are considered as predictors of bullying. The Wellness and Equality scales measure those dimensions of the school environment that, according to our hypothesis, reduce the risk of bullying and, therefore, present negative predictors of bullying.

3. *Survey on Bullying Cases:* To identify bullying cases, we apply Mynard and Joseph's[4] multidimensional peer-victimization scale (form A), which is meant to assess direct and indirect victimization.[5] The scale contains forty-five actions and points to four types of victimization: physical victimization, verbal victimization, social manipulation, and property

---

[4] H. Mynard and S. Joseph, 2000.

[5] We applied the version of the given test adapted by Elene Chomakhidze and Mari Kikalishvili in 2018.

infringement. To measure *physical victimization,* we offer teenagers three possible answers—never, rarely, often—to evaluate such statements as, "I'm being attacked," "I'm being kicked," "I'm being hurt physically," "I'm being beaten." *Verbal victimization* is measured by the following statements: "I'm being mocked for my appearance," "I'm being made fun of," "I'm being made fun of for no reason," and, "I'm being shouted at." To measure *social manipulation,* teenagers are asked to assess the frequency of such cases as, "They are trying to ruin my relationship with my friends," "They turn my friends against me," "They do not talk to me," "They influence others not to talk to me." Finally, the test also provides information about *property infringement.* In particular, questions related to property ownership. Particularly, whether someone takes their belongings without permission, breaks their belongings, or intentionally spoils them.

By means of this test, the forms of violence, and consequently victimization and their frequency, are determined by peers.

Sample Description and Frame Formation

Based on the literature analyzed, we can assume that deviant behaviors most often occur in high school classes. Consequently, we selected the participants from ninth to twelfth grades for our survey and asked them to fill out the questionnaires.

Taking into account the literature analysis and our hypotheses, we identified survey variables that could impact the attitudes reflected in our hypotheses as additional variables. These variables are:

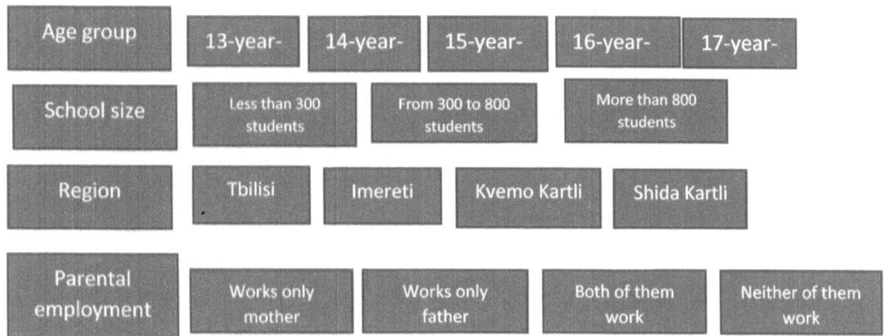

Chart of additional variables.

Thus, the sample of our survey was limited to students from ninth to twelfth grades in Georgian secondary schools.

We applied accessible sampling[6] in forming the sampling framework for the survey. Through the social network, we contacted the principals of various schools and the representatives of resource centers. They were provided with information about the survey, shared the SurveyMonkey link, and provided an official letter of support from the Ministry of Education, Science, Culture, and Sports of Georgia. The survey lasted for six weeks, and 1,422 teenagers participated in it.

---

[6] The specific schools identified for the survey were selected in consultation with the Ministry of Education, Science, Culture, and Sports of Georgia. But due to the COVID-19 pandemic and restrictions, we were unable to enter the schools. Given the epidemic situation, all general education institutions switched to remote mode, and we had to use the accessible sampling method for the survey.

SURVEY RESULTS

As mentioned previously, a total of 1,422 high school students participated in the survey, of which 931 were girls and 491 were boys (see table 1).

	Number	Percent
Girls	931	65.5
Boys	491	34.5
Total	1422	100.0

The interviewed respondents by their school sizes are presented in table 2.

School size	Number	Percent
Less than 300 students	41	2.9
From 300 to 800 students	502	35.6
More than 800 students	869	61.5
Total	1412	100.0

The age distribution of the survey participants is presented in table 3.

Age	Frequency	Percent
13-year- olds	29	2.1
14-year- olds	298	21.1
15-year- olds	441	31.2

16-year- olds	431	30.5
17-year- olds	213	15.1
Total	1412	100.0

The number of respondents interviewed in the regions is given in table 4.

Region	Number	Percent
Tbilisi	865	60.83%
Imereti	91	6.40%
Kvemo Kartli	191	13.43%
Shida Kartli	229	16.10%
Other regions	46	3.23%
Total	1422	100.00%

The survey results were processed by SPSS statistics 21. To test the hypothesis, we constructed a hierarchical regression model in which, pursuant to the hypothesis, the victimization scale was defined as a dependent variable. It was important for the survey to determine the impact of two polar-type school culture indicators, such as "wellness" and "equality" on the one hand, and "threat" and "isolation" on the other, on the victimization indicator. In the model pursuant to the hypothesis, the "aggression" is also an independent variable.

A linear hierarchical model was used, the components of which were the dependent variable—victimization scale—and the independent variables—four types of school culture separately, as well as age, gender, school size, parental work indicators, and region.

At the initial stage of the analysis, aggression was not considered in the model. Only the weight of the impact of school culture types and additional variables, regardless of the indicator of aggression, is measured on the victimization scale. The results of the performed regression analysis are presented in tables 5 and 6.

Model Summary				
Model	R	R Square	Adjusted R Square	Std. Error of the Estimate
1	.559[a]	.313	.308	6.25833

Coefficients[a]						
Model		Unstandardized Coefficients		Standardized Coefficients	t	Sig.
		B	Std. Error	Beta		
1	(Constant)	46.516	2.016		23.068	.000
	Isolation (sk_g)	.605	.117	.133	5.159	.000
	Wellness (sk_k)	-.508	.115	-.116	-4.433	.000
	Threat (sk_s)	.839	.064	.371	13.048	.000
	Equality (sk_t)	-.426	.123	-.084	-3.481	.001
	13 -year-old (starting point)	**.000**		**.000**		
	14 -year-old	2.185	1.227	.118	1.781	.075
	15 -year-old	2.590	1.209	.160	2.143	.032
	16 -year-old	2.121	1.207	.129	1.757	.079
	17 -year-old	1.370	1.248	.065	1.097	.273
	Girl	-.721	.357	-.046	-2.021	.043
	Works only father (starting point)	**.000**		**.000**		
	Works only mother	.147	.577	.007	.255	.798
	Both work	.085	.412	.006	.207	.836
	Neither of them work	3.130	.855	.089	3.659	.000
	Tbilisi (starting point)	**0.000**		**.000**		
	Kvemo Kartli	.014	.533	.001	.025	.980
	Shida Kartli	**1.432**	**.498**	**.070**	**2.876**	**.004**
	Imereti	1.166	.731	.038	1.594	.111
	Other regions	**4.679**	**1.041**	**.104**	**4.496**	**.000**

School size - less than 300-students (starting point)	0.000		.000		
School size – from 300 to 800 students	.580	1.047	.037	.554	.580
School size - more than 800 students	1.138	1.033	.073	1.102	.271
a. Dependent Variable vs Victimization Scale					

As a result of the regression analysis, it was found that the determination coefficient is rather high ($R = .559$), which indicates that the correlation between the victimization scale and the independent variables participating in the model is quite high. Consequently, we can assume that the model developed by us efficiently explains 31.1 percent of victimization measured. In other words, almost one third of revealed victimization is conditioned by the impact of the variables assumed by us. Particularly, the impact of most variables participating in the model turned out to be statistically significant. All four variables of school culture (isolation, wellness, threat, and equality) are predictors of victimization. Table 7 demonstrates that experiencing isolation ($\beta = .133$, $p = .000$) and threat ($\beta = .371$, $p = .000$) exacerbates victimization, while wellness ($\beta = -0.116$, $p = .000$) and equality ($\beta = -.084$, $p = .001$) reduces victimization.

The variables age, gender, parental employment indicator, and region (Shida Kartli) also enjoy statistically significant predictive values. As for the variable school size, it was not found to be statistically significant, meaning its impact on the victimization indicator was not confirmed.

If we remove statistically insignificant parameters from the model table, we get the table of the following independent variables that impact the victimization indicator.

Coefficients[a]					
Model	Unstandardized Coefficients		Standardized Coefficients	t	Sig.
	B	Std. Error	Beta		
1 (Constant)	46.516	2.016		23.068	0
Isolation (sk_g)	0.605	0.117	0.133	5.159	0.000
Wellness (sk_k)	-0.508	0.115	-0.116	-4.433	0.000
Threat (sk_s)	0.839	0.064	0.371	13.048	0.000
Equality (sk_t)	-0.426	0.123	-0.084	-3.481	0.001
15-year-old	2.59	1.209	0.16	2.143	0.032
Girl	-0.721	0.357	-0.046	-2.021	0.043
Neither of them work	3.13	0.855	0.089	3.659	0.000
Shida Kartli	**1.432**	**0.498**	**0.07**	**2.876**	**0.004**
Other regions	**4.679**	**1.041**	**0.104**	**4.496**	**0.000**

a. Dependent Variable vs. Victimization Scale

Obtained results practically give us the risk factors that should be considered when working on bullying. This issue is discussed in more detail below.

It is also interesting for the survey to analyze the weight of predictor impact. To represent it clearly, we converted the magnitude of the beta coefficients into percentages (see table 8).

Predictors	*Beta*	*Absolute magnitude of Beta coefficient*	*Share in percentage*	
Isolation (sk_g)	*0.14*	*0.13*	*11.61%*	***63.39%***
Wellness (sk_k)	*-0.12*	*0.12*	*10.71%*	
Threat (sk_s)	*0.37*	*0.37*	*33.04%*	
Equality (sk_t)	*-0.09*	*0.09*	*8.04%*	

15 years old	0.12		0.16	14.29%	36.61%
Girl	-0.04		0.05	4.46%	
Neither of them work	**0.1**		**0.1**	**8.93%**	
Shida Kartli	**0.05**		**0.1**	**8.93%**	

As obvious from the table, the most influential predictors of bullying behavior are the variables of school culture. They comprise almost two-thirds (63 percent) of conditionality. The most powerful factor that affects the victimization scale is the type of school culture, specifically "threat." Its share of impact comprises one-third (33.04 percent) of the total impact. The share of impact of the type of school culture "isolation" is 11.61 percent of the total. Both variables are positive predictors of victimization (bullying). In other words, they reinforce the indicator of victimization. The types of school culture "wellness" and "equality" are negative predictors of victimization, which means they weaken/reduce the indicator of victimization. "Wellness" is 10.11 percent of the total impact, and the impact of "equality" is 8.04 percent.

The impacts of other additional factors, particularly age, gender, parental employment, and region factors, are slightly more than one third (36.61 percent). Let us consider each of them separately. The impact weight of fifteen-year-olds is 14.29 percent of the total impact. Two important predictors of victimization are neither parent working and being in the Shida Kartli region. Each makes a relatively small but positive contribution to the high indicator of victimization (8.93 percent). The regression analysis also revealed that the gender is a small victimization predictor though with reliable impact. In particular, the variable "girl" is a negative predictor, and the weight of its impact on victimization indicator is 4.46 percent of the total impact.

Thus, the model showed that 31.1 percent of the bullying cases are conditioned by the variables that we assumed and outlined in the survey.

Hence, as the results show, the impact of school culture compared to other variables is much greater, which is consistent with our hypothesis. It is obvious that school culture is a strong predictor of bullying behaviors. By analyzing the interactions of these variables, we can easily talk about the psychological model of bullying.

In order to further improve the model discussed previously, at the next stage, while constructing a hierarchical model of regression analysis, in addition to school culture, we also took into account the indicator of aggression, since our hypothesis also suggests that a safe school culture type tends to reduce victimization despite the level of aggression. An unsafe one, on the contrary, demonstrates an increase in cases of bullying. Hence, we made an assumption that even in the presence of aggression, if school culture does not provide the instrumental possibilities for realizing the set, victimization is less likely to occur. For this purpose, we constructed a new model of regression. To do this, we first measured the correlation.

Correlations				
		sk_g isolation	sk_k wellness	sk_s threat	sk_t equality
bd agression	Pearson Correlation	.184**	-.269**	.342**	-.204**
	Sig. (2-tailed)	.000	.000	.000	.000
	N	1428	1428	1430	1428
**. Correlation is significant at the 0.01 level (2-tailed).				

Table 9 demonstrates that aggression has a small though statistically significant positive relationship with the indicators of the types of school culture "isolation" and "threat," as well as a small but statistically significant negative relationship with school culture types of "wellness" and "equality." This fact is consistent with our hypothesis.

While constructing the regression model, we first introduced the background (mean) indicator of aggression, which is the mean of the aggression calculated based on the school variables. We then constructed the regression model taking into consideration only the mean indicator of aggression at the initial stage and later adding the variables of the school culture types listed previously (see tables 10 and 11).

Model Summary				
Model	R	R Square	Adjusted R Square	Std. Error of the Estimate
1	.089[a]	.008	.007	7.78671
a. Predictors: (Constant), bd_mean				

Coefficients[a]						
Model		Unstandardized Coefficients		Standardized Coefficients	t	Sig.
		B	Std. Error	Beta		
1	(Constant)	43.214	1.969		21.943	.000
	bd_mean	.175	.050	.089	3.500	.000
a. Dependent Variable: vs Victimization scale						

The analysis revealed that the mean indicator of aggression is a weak though statistically significant predictor of victimization. At the following stage, the variables of school culture types were added to the given model (see tables 12 and 13). The analysis demonstrated that inclusion of school culture indicators in the model led to weakening of the predictive weight of the indicator of the background aggression and loss of statistical significance.

Model Summary				
Model	R	R Square	Adjusted R Square	Std. Error of the Estimate
1	.543[a]	.295	.293	6.57443
a. Predictors: (Constant), sk_t Equality, bd_mean, sk_g Isolation, sk_k Wellness, sk_s Threat				

Coefficients[a]						
Model		Unstandardized Coefficients		Standardized Coefficients	t	Sig.
		B	Std. Error	Beta		
1	(Constant)	51.144	2.145		23.842	.000
	sk_g Isolation	.635	.116	.135	5.471	.000
	sk_k Welness	-.484	.115	-.106	-4.212	.000
	sk_s Threat	.856	.062	.368	13.845	.000
	sk_t Equality	-.484	.121	-.093	-3.994	.000
	bd_mean	-.047	.043	-.024	-1.084	.279
a. Dependent Variable: vs Victimisation Scale						

For further analysis in order to test the hypotheses, we calculated the combined variable of school culture and aggression based on the correlation, which was expressed as the product of these two variables. To obtain the values for statistical analysis, we changed the "wellness" and "equality" signs (since it has a negative relationship with the aggression indicator) and adjusted cross product.

View table 14 of relevant products that follows.

Model Summary				
Model	R	R Square	Adjusted R Square	Std. Error of the Estimate
1	.591[a]	0.349	0.338	6.13139

Hence, we obtained new variables and by means of them, we constructed a new model.

The regression analysis showed that the variables derived from the combination of school culture and aggression provide a more improved model that better explains victimization. The coefficient of determination is even higher ($R = .591$), and, respectively, explains 33.8 percent of victimization. The regression model obtained as a result of statistical analysis is presented in table 15.

	Unstandardized Coefficients		Standardized Coefficients	t	Sig.
	B	Std. Error	Beta		
(Constant)	48.81	1.161		42.041	0
Isolation (sk_g)	-.217	.465	-.048	-.466	.641
Wellness (sk_k)	.651	.358	.149	1.818	.099
Threat(sk_s)	-.046	.211	-.021	-.219	.827
Equality (sk_t)	-1.013	.436	-.202	-2.326	.02
Isolation and aggression (sk_g_bd)	.021	.011	.214	1.922	.05
Wellness and aggression (sk_k_bd)	-.026	.009	-.28	-3.041	.002
Threat and aggression (sk_s_bd)	.02	.005	.443	4.018	.000
Equality and aggression (sk_t_bd)	.014	.011	.135	1.333	.183

This time, school culture variables "isolation," "wellness," and "threat" separately did not give a statistically significant result as when considered along with aggression. So the advantages of our new model are obvious. The table shows that the variables "isolation and aggression," "wellness and aggression," and "threat and aggression" have predictive value of high reliability. Consequently, $\beta = .214$, $p = .05$; $\beta = -.28$, $p = .002$; $\beta = 443$, $p = .000$, and the variable "equality with aggression" is not the victimization predictor ($\beta = .135$, $p = .183$). However, the variable of school culture "equality" separately is a reliable negative predictor of victimization ($\beta = -.202$, $p = .02$). It seems that it is unable to compete with aggression and, respectively, in combination with the variable of aggression fails to have a negative impact on the victimization scale.

At the following stage we introduced additional variables interesting for us and received the results found in table 16.

Model Summary				
Model	R	R Square	Adjusted R Square	Std. Error of the Estimate
1	.591[a]	.350	.339	6.12720

Coefficients[a]					
Model	Unstandardized Coefficients		Standardized Coefficients	t	Sig
	B	Std. Error	Beta-		
(Constant)	45.738	1.987		23.022	.000
Isolation (sk_g)	-.228	.469	-.050	-.486	.627
Wellness (sk_k)	.685	.361	-.157	1.897	.058
Threat(sk_s)	.046	.214	.020	.215	.830
Equality (sk_t)	-1.166	.440	-.231	-2.652	.008
Isolation and aggression (sk_g_bd)	**.020**	**.011**	**.198**	**1.780**	**.045**
Wellness and aggression (sk_k_bd)	**.028**	**.009**	**-.302**	**3.258**	**.001**
Threat and aggression (sk_s_bd)	**.018**	**.005**	**.403**	**3.620**	**.000**
Equality and aggression (sk_t_bd)	**-.019**	**.011**	**-.182**	**-1.792**	**.073**
13 -year-old (starting point)	**.000**		**.000**		
14 -year-old	2.223	1.207	.120	1.842	.066
15 -year-old-year-old	**2.587**	**1.189**	**.159**	**2.176**	**.030**
16 -year-old	2.134	1.187	.130	1.798	.072
17 -year-old	1.404	1.228	.067	1.143	.253
Girl	-.539	.352	-.034	-1.535	.125
Works only father (starting pont)	**.000**		**.000**		
Works only mother	.182	.568	.008	.321	.748
Both work	.145	.405	.009	.357	.721

Neither of them work	3.033	.842	.086	3.604	.000
Tbilisi (starting point)	**0.000**		**.000**		
Kvemo Kartli	-.093	.528	-.004	-.176	.860
Shida Kartli	1.365	.491	.067	2.782	.005
Imereti	.902	.720	.029	1.252	.211
Other regions	4.804	1.025	.107	4.689	.000
School size - Less than 300 students (starting point)	**0.000**		**.000**		
School size - From 300 to 800 students	.750	1.031	.048	.727	.467
School size - more than 800 students	1.322	1.017	.085	1.300	.194
a. Dependent Variable: vs Victimization scale					

Here we thought it would be interesting to analyze the weight of impact of predictors. For a better demonstration, we converted the value of beta coefficient into percentage (see table 18).

	Beta	Absolute value of Beta coefficient	Share in percentage		
sk_t equality	-0.231	0.231	14.87%	14.87%	**73.02%**
sk_g_bd isolation and aggression	**0.198**	0.198	12.75%	58.15%	
sk_k_bd wellness and aggression	**-0.302**	0.302	19.45%		
sk_s_bd threat and aggression	**0.403**	0.403	25.95%		
age_15 -year-old	**0.159**	0.159	10.24%	**26.98%**	
Neither of them work	**0.086**	0.086	5.54%		
Shida Kartli	0.067	0.067	4.31%		
Other regions	0.107	0.107	6.89%		
		1.553	100.00%	**100%**	

As the results of the hierarchical regression model above show, the variables of educational space—such as the combination of school culture and class aggression level—explain 73.02 percent of the total impact, 34 percent revealed through regression.

To clearly illustrate the regression model constructed in terms of the survey, we present diagram 1, in which the X axis represents the assessed value of victimization in terms of the values of the variables participating in the student regression, and Y represents the victimization value for students.

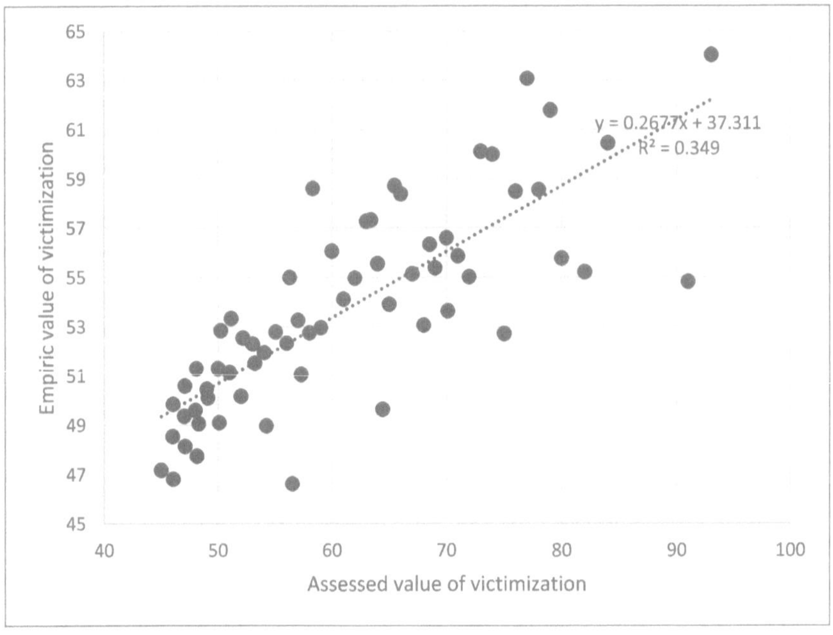

Among the predictors affecting bullying behavior, the school culture variables, in combination with the aggression variable, are the most influential. They comprise almost four-fifths (73.02 percent) of conditionality. Of these, the combined variable of aggression and school culture type "threat" has the strongest impact on the victimization scale. The share of its impact is more than one fourth

(25.95 percent) of the total impact. The share of the impact of the combined variable of aggression and the school culture type "wellness" is 19.45 percent of the total impact. However, the latter, unlike the former, has a negative impact on the victimization scale. In other words, if the former variable enhances the victimization indicator, the latter reduces it. In terms of its strength, the school culture type variable "equality" is in third place; its predictive weight is 14.87 percent of the total impact. However, as shown previously, this variable, in combination with aggression, loses its power, indicating that the similar school culture type at the background of high aggression fails to have a mitigating effect on victimization. In terms of predictive power, next comes the combined variable of aggression and the school culture type "isolation," the impact weight of which is 12.75 percent of the total impact.

The impacts of additional factors are slightly more than a quarter (26.98 percent). In particular, these variables are: age, parental employment, and region factors. Unlike the previous model, the gender and sixteen-year-old variables no longer have predictive value. Obviously, it is due to application of more-refined measurements, which implied taking account of the aggression variable in the model. It should be also noted that the variable "other regions" was added to the predictors of the victimization[7] variable.

Thus, an important finding for us is the following: Our survey showed that 73 percent of teenager victimization is explained by

---

[7] The study identified the following regional variables: "Tbilisi," "Imereti," "Mtskheta-Mtianeti," "Kvemo Kartli," "Shida Kartli," and the rest of regions, which are combined in the variable "Other Regions."

the emotional background conditioned by the classroom and school culture. Emotional background implies feelings of anxiety, threat, and tension. Our survey showed that the likelihood of becoming a victim—victimhood—is high among those teenagers who think that interference, disdain, name-calling, ridiculing, fighting, swearing, and cursing are acceptable in their classes. Consequently, when a teenager experiences a sense of threat, he or she develops physical, psychological, or social symptoms that make the student vulnerable to bullying. Our survey showed that the sense of victimhood depends on one more factor, and that is the sense of isolation. When a student experiences actual tension—he or she does not play or make friends with classmates, nobody supports him or her, fighting is frequent in the class, attending classes is assessed as an uninteresting and unpleasant condition, the student does not feel well—such a feeling in combination with aggression reinforces victimhood of the student.

The picture is opposite when we researched the polar characteristics of "threat" and "isolation." The results clearly demonstrate that a school culture that is oriented on adhering to the rules of communication and mutual respect in the group reduces the likelihood of teenagers becoming victims. Consequently, when teenagers feel they will not be disturbed and that no one will touch their items left in the classroom or corridor, when they feel teachers are happy to enter their classrooms, and when a fight is always a surprise, then they have a sense of well-being. And according to our survey, even in combination with aggression, they are less likely to become a victim.

The result obtained by the combination of two variables—aggression and equality—is worthy of analysis. As already mentioned, a sense of equality at school (that is, when relationships are equal, when summoning a student to the principal means that he or she will be praised, when the student freely enter another classroom to meet with friends during breaks) reduces the likelihood of becoming a victim. However, in combination with aggression, this variable failed to demonstrate a positive (reducing) effect on victimization. Consequently, as we have seen the sense of wellness, regardless of the level of aggression, has reduced the likelihood of becoming a victim, it is desirable to promote such school cultures that enhance the sense of wellness among teenagers. Consequently, we can conclude that when there is a benevolent environment in the school, aggression no longer becomes the determinant of behavior. In such a case, aggression can no longer interfere with the sense of equality, and therefore, this feeling will not be suppressed.

The results showed the display of bullying requires a combination of three components: personal aggression, the object required for the realization of aggression, and the possibilities and conditions available in the environment. In compliance with our hypothesis, it is the unity of these factors that makes bullying behavior possible. Therefore, our survey clearly demonstrated that for bullying to occur, there must be aggression, an object of aggression (victim), and an environment that will allow the bully to display aggression. Based on this result, we can define bullying as behavior arising from a unity of factors, not as an action caused by the influence of individual factors. Consequently, our leading hypothesis—that bullying occurs in the presence of aggression, a potential victim, and an environment conducive for this behavior—has been confirmed. We can conclude an environment for bullying is present in a school if it evokes the sense of threat or isolation among the teenagers. Consequently, there is a low chance of bullying in schools where teenagers experience wellness and equality. Therefore, we can say that Dimitri Uznadze's theory of set well explains the psychological mechanism of bullying.

Accordingly, the results showed that school culture can be both a risk factor for bullying to occur and its antipredictor, which creates an important picture for educational psychology and related disciplines. The analysis of these results explains the psychological model of bullying on the one hand, and on the other, we can identify school resources that, when adequately applied in schools, will reduce the risks of bullying. (This issue will be discussed in more detail in chapter 7.)

While analyzing the regression model, in addition to school variables, we also identified statistically significant additional variables. Let us consider additional variables separately. The impact weight of fifteen-year-olds comprises 10.24 percent of the total impact. The impact weight of the variable "other regions" on the victimization factor is 6.89 percent of the total impact. A significant predictor of victimization is "neither of parents work," whose impact weight on the victimization factor is 5.54 percent of the total impact. A relatively smaller but positive contribution to the high victimization factor is made by the Shida Kartli region: The impact weight of this region is 4.31 percent of the total impact.

The variables that have predictive value on the victimization variable and their share of impact for clearer observation are presented graphically in graphic 1.

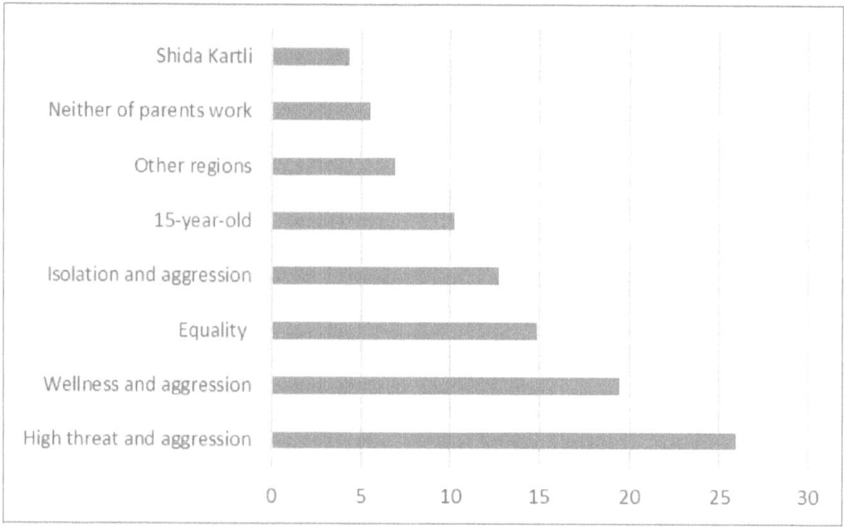

Hence, based on survey results, we can assume that the occurrence of bullying cases is more anticipated:

- Among fifteen-year-olds.
- In classes where the school culture is "threat" type, especially in those classes where the aggression background is high.
- In classes where the school culture is "isolation" type, especially in those classes where the aggression background is high.
- Where there are children whose both parents do not work.
- Shida Kartliʋ schools represent a high-threat group.

At the following stage of analysis, we found it important to analyze the school culture types and the victimization indicators in terms of the parameters we identified. For this purpose, we calculated the indexes of school culture types "isolation," "wellness," "threat," "equality," and the "aggression" and "victimization scale" by means of an answer key. To obtain comparable data, we converted them into normalized values. This enabled us to compare the scales.

Normalized values, or the Z point, is defined by the following formula: $Z = \dfrac{x - \overline{x}}{S_x}$, where x is the variable value.

$\overline{x}$ is the mean value of the variable.

S_x is the standard deviation of the variable.

In terms of the variables given above, we applied the ANOVA method to analyze and compare the means of school culture types and aggression and victimization scales indicators.

Table 19 displays mean data of school culture types by school size, aggression and victimization scales indicators and significance of the difference among them.

Mean						
Size of the School	sk_g isolation	sk_k wellness	sk_s threat	sk_t equality	bd aggression	vs victimization scale
less than 300 students	0.12	0.14	0.01	-0.05	-0.08	-0.10
from 300 to 800 students	-0.03	0.12	-0.14	0.10	-0.05	-0.08
more than 800 students	-0.01	-0.07	0.08	-0.04	0.04	0.03
sig	0.62	**0.02**	**0.000**	**0.045**	0.25	0.08

Based on the data analysis, we can conclude that in terms of school culture types—"wellness," "threat," and "equality"—as well as of summarized indicators, we have different pictures in schools of different size, and this difference is statistically significant.

Particularly, the mean of normalized values of the school culture "wellness" in the schools with less than three hundred students is high (higher than mean, since the mean of normalized value is 0) and comprises 0.14. The mean of normalized value is also high (0.12) in the schools with a student population of three hundred to eight hundred. In schools with more than eight hundred students, the mean of normalized value of school culture type "wellness" acquires negative value that points to the fact that the mean of normalized value of school culture type "wellness" in such schools is relatively low (lower than mean, since the mean of normalized value is 0). The difference between means is statistically significant: $F(2) = 6.475$, $sig = 0.002$.

The mean of the normalized value of school culture type "threat" in the school where there are less than three hundred students is actually mean (0.01). In the schools with the number of students from three hundred to eight hundred, this indicator reduces even more and acquires a negative value (0.14); hence, it is less than a mean value. Regarding schools with more than eight hundred students, the mean of normalized value of school culture "threat" acquires the highest value, 0.08. Thus, we can conclude that both in the schools with relatively fewer students and with relatively multinumber students, the indicator of school culture type "threat" is higher. And in the average-size school, where there are from three hundred to eight hundred students, the indicator of school culture type "threat" is the lowest, The difference between means is statistically significant: $F(2) = 8.550$, $sig = 0.000$.

The mean of the normalized value of school culture type "equality" in the school, when there are less than three hundred students is relatively low (lower than mean) and comprises –0.05; the mean of normalized indicators is also low (–0.04) in schools with more than eight hundred students. As for schools with student populations from three hundred to eight hundred, the mean of the normalized value of school culture type "equality" is rather high (0.1). The difference between means is statistically significant $F(2) = 3.045$, $sig = 0.048$.

The differences between the means of indicators of different school culture types by school size are given in graphics 2, 3, 4.

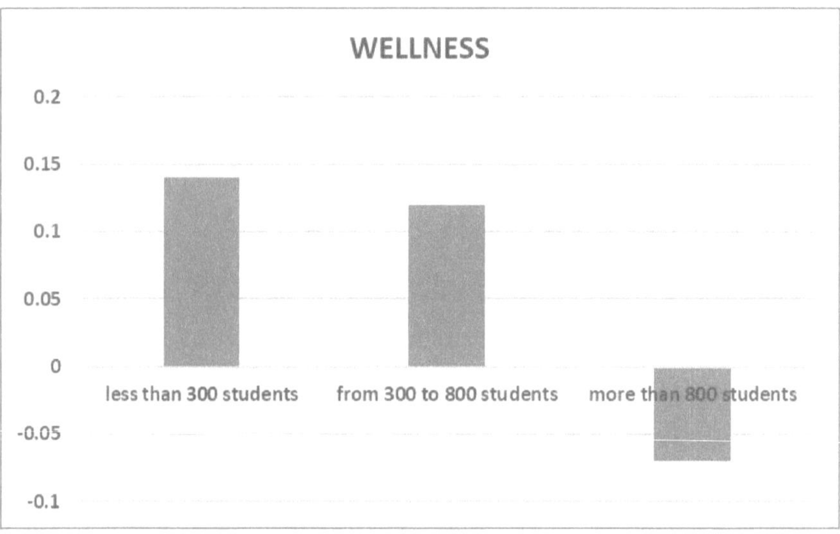

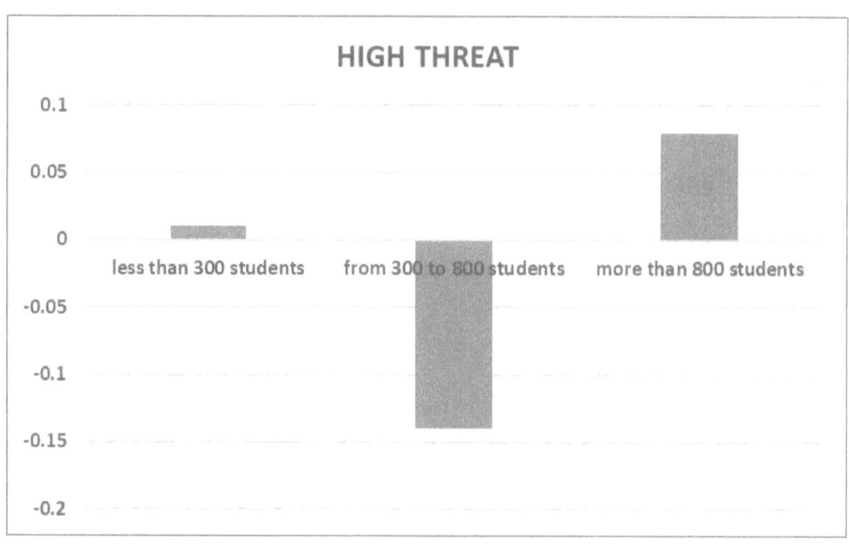

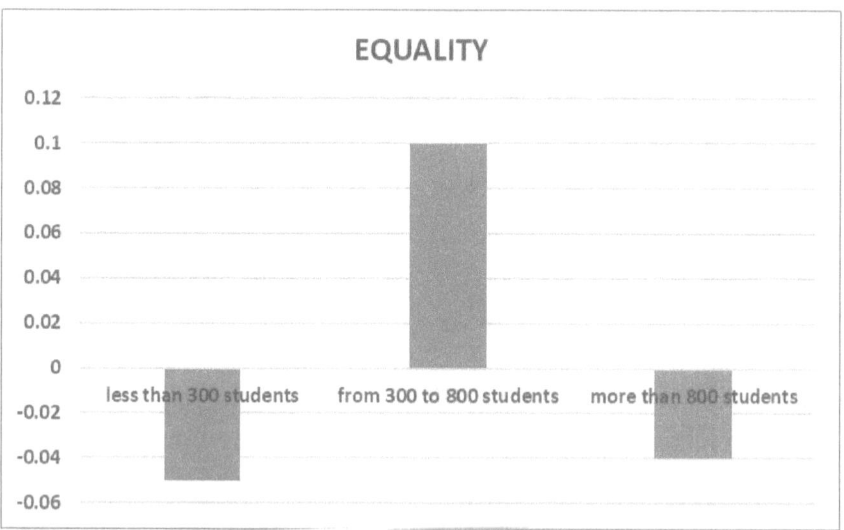

As it became clear, the number of students in the school (that is, school size) can be considered a factor of the occurrence of bullying. The analysis of the results of the survey enables us to conclude that teenagers feel most comfortable when the number of students in the school ranges from three hundred to eight hundred students. In schools of this size, teenagers demonstrated the highest levels of wellness and equality and the lowest level of risk. Consequently, we can state that in schools with an average number of students, we encounter an environment in which everything is based on mutual respect, adherence to communication rules, and equality, unlike what is found in small or large schools. We believe the results obtained will be valuable information for the education policy planning process.

We received interesting results while analyzing the differences between the means of the school culture types and victimization scale indicators by parental employment. ANOVA analysis showed statistically significant different means by the school culture types "isolation" and "wellness," as well as by parental employment on the victimization scale (see table 20).

q0173 my parents work	sk_g isolation	sk_k wellness	sk_s threat	sk_t equality	bd aggression	vs victimization scale
1 only mother works	0.23	-0.19	0.10	-0.08	0.05	0.09
2 only father works	-0.10	0.10	-0.10	0.03	-0.02	-0.09
3 both work	-0.05	0.01	0.01	0.04	0.00	-0.04
4 neither of them work	0.22	0.07	0.00	-0.03	-0.01	0.41
sig	*0.00*	*0.012*	0.12	0.50	0.86	*0.00*

It should be noted that the mean indicator of "isolation" is high in the case of students who report that "only mother works" or "neither of parents work" (0.23 and 0.22, respectively). And in the case of students whose both parents work, "isolation" is relatively low (–0.5). It is even lower when only the father works: "Only father works": $F(3) = 6.520$, $p = 0.000$. It is interesting to note that the mean indicator of "wellness" is relatively low (–0.19) for those students whose "only mother works," and highest for the students whose "only father works" (0.10). In the remaining cases, when both parents work or neither work, the wellness indicator is actually mean, 0.01 and 0.07, respectively: $F(3) = 3.658$, $p = 0.012$).

While analyzing the difference between means of the victimization scale in terms of parental work—$F(3 = 6.028$, $p = 0.000$—it was found that the mean indicator of victimization is particularly high when neither parent works. In other cases of parental employment, we obtained more or less mean indicators of victimization.

The differences between means of different types of school culture by parental employment are presented in the graphics 5, 6, and 7.

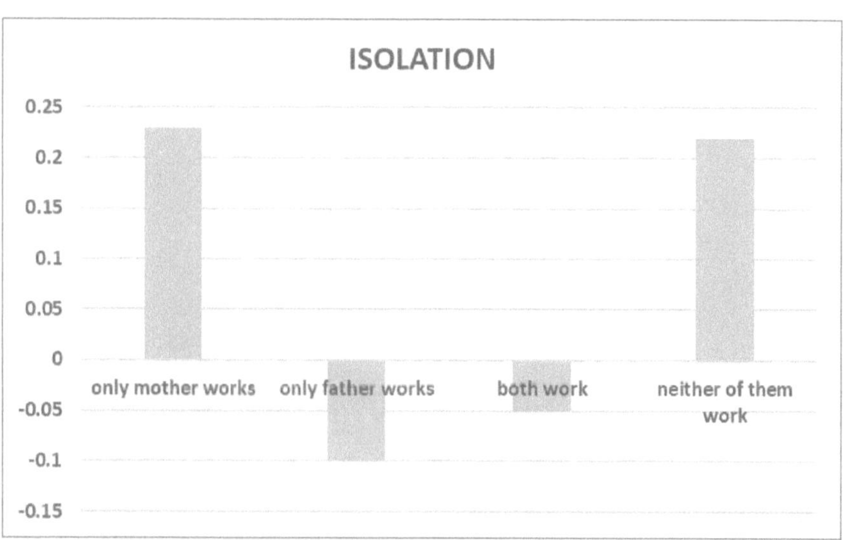

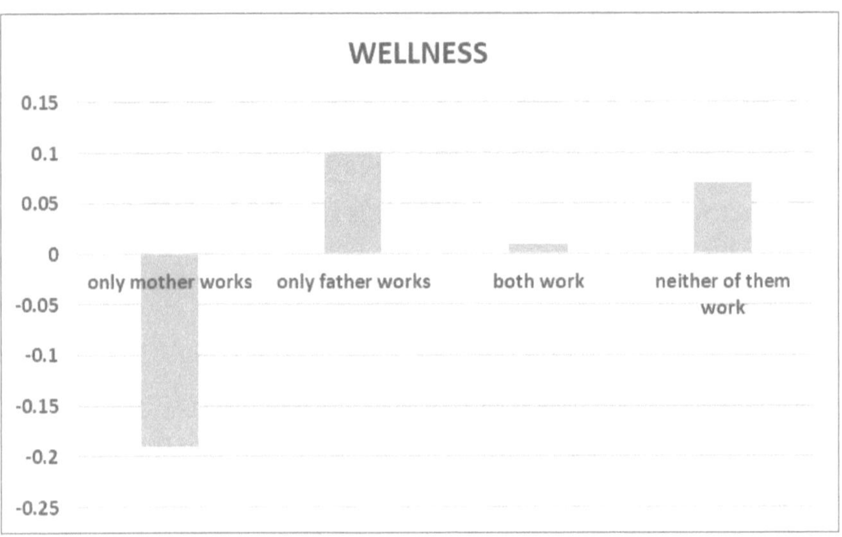

The results obtained for the parental employment indicator are interesting to consider in terms of the sociocultural aspect. We can state that teenagers whose only mother works or neither parent work experience real strain, loneliness, and isolation at school. Consequently, the students whose only father or both parents are employed feel less isolated. We can also assume that the presence of their mothers is an important factor for whether teenagers experience the sense of wellness. According to the survey, a teenager feels the lowest benevolence when only the mother works. In this context, the results of the victimization scale are all the more interesting. Students feel victimized when neither of the parents work, although the likelihood of victimization is also high when only the mother is employed.

Certainly, school culture should not be seen as a system of values separate from one's society. We should always remember what gender or cultural stereotypes are nurtured within that society and are reflected in school culture. If a teenager thinks that he or she lives in a reality unacceptable to society, it will inevitably affect the perception of himself or herself in relation to the environment. A person, and even more so a teenager, has a greater chance of developing an adaptation problem and feeling of isolation or being victimized when he or she feels the current situation (when mother is employed and father is unemployed) runs opposite to established societal values or gender roles that offered a family model in which the man is the breadwinner and the woman the caregiver. It seems that in our society, this stereotype is still clearly maintained, at least at the level of consciousness.

Thus, we can assume these results are influenced by our gender consciousness, which we know is part of the social consciousness and determines the rules of cohabitation and relationships between women and men. Therefore, we believe this result will be significant for those involved in the research of gender consciousness.

We also received interesting results when analyzing the differences in the mean values of school culture types by student age groups (table

21). The ANOVA analysis showed statistically significant differences in the means of values of school culture types "isolation," "threat," and "equality."

It should be noted that the mean value of "isolation" is high among seventeen-year-old students (0.21) and below mean among fourteen-year-old students (–.015). In other age groups, this type of school culture is mean or below mean (see table 21). The differences between means are statistically significant: $F(4) = 4.347$, $p = 0.002$. A statistically significant difference was revealed between the mean values of the school culture type "threat" in different age categories: $F(4) = 2.485$, $p = 0.042$. Particularly, the mean value of "isolation" is high among seventeen-year-olds (0.18), while in other age groups, this value of school culture is almost mean (slightly above or below mean).

As for the mean value of the type of school culture of "equality," it is higher than the mean among sixteen-year-old students (0.13) as well as among thirteen-year-old students (0.09), but it is below mean among fourteen-year-old students (–0.10). In other age groups, these data are slightly higher or lower than mean: $F(4) = 2.615$, $p = 0.034$.

Mean					
AGE I am	sk_g isolation	sk_k wellness	sk_s threat	sk_t equality	bd aggression	vs victimization scale
13 years old	-0.02	0.04	-0.06	0.09	0.00	-0.27
14 years old	-0.15	0.01	-0.07	-0.10	-0.07	-0.05
15 years old	-0.03	0.03	-0.04	-0.03	-0.06	0.03
16 years old	0.00	0.03	0.02	0.13	0.06	-0.01

17 years old	0.21	-0.15	0.18	-0.01	0.11	0.02
sig	***0.002***	0.21	***0.042***	***0.034***	0.10	0.42

The difference between the means of the values of different types of school culture by the age of the students is presented in graphics 8, 9, and 10.

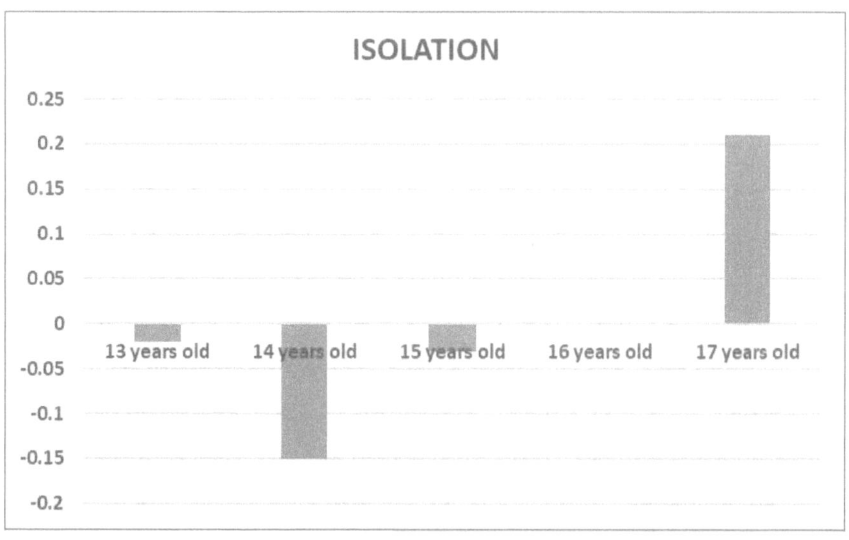

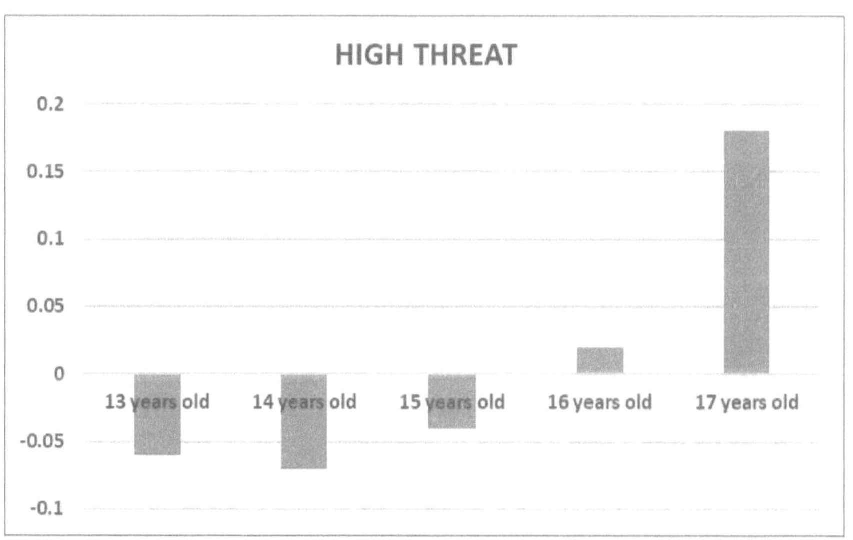

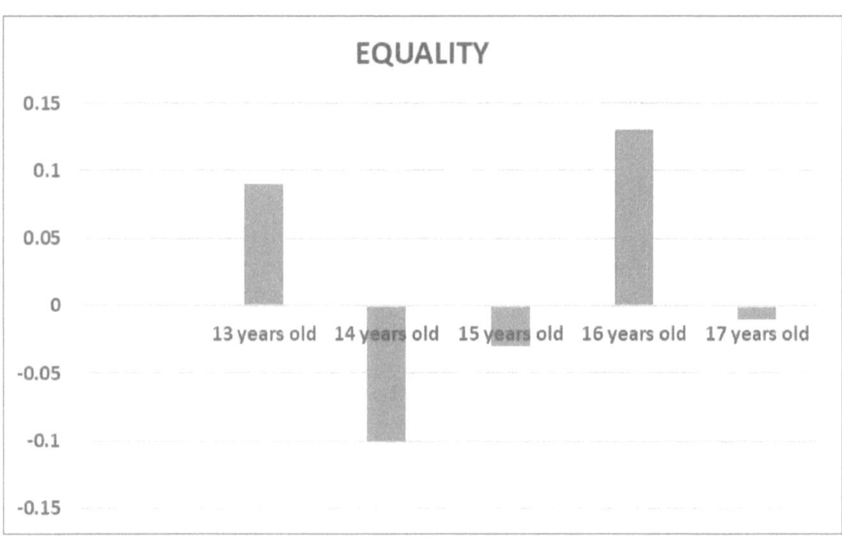

We received valuable results when we analyzed differences in the mean values of the school culture types by student gender (table 22). The ANOVA analysis showed statistically significant differences in the mean values of the school culture types on the "threat" and "victimization" scales: F (4) = 9.310, p = 0.002 and F (4) = 10.395, p = 0.001, respectively. It is particularly interesting to note that the "threat" is higher among girls (0.05) than among boys (–0.11), as well as the mean value of "victimization" (see 0.05 and –0.013, respectively).

Mean						
sex I am a	sk_g isolation	sk_k wellness	sk_s threat	sk_t equality	bd aggression	vs victimization scale
girl	0.02	0.00	0.05	-0.02	0.03	0.05
2 boy	-0.07	0.02	-0.11	0.07	-0.06	-0.13
Sig.	0.09	0.75	0.002	0.08	0.12	0.001

The differences between the means of the values of different types of school culture by gender of the students are presented in the graphics 11 and 12.

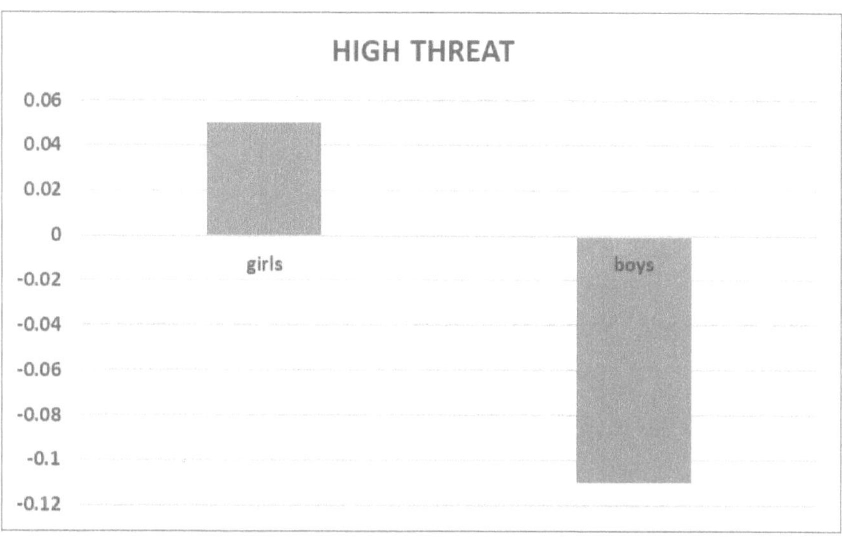

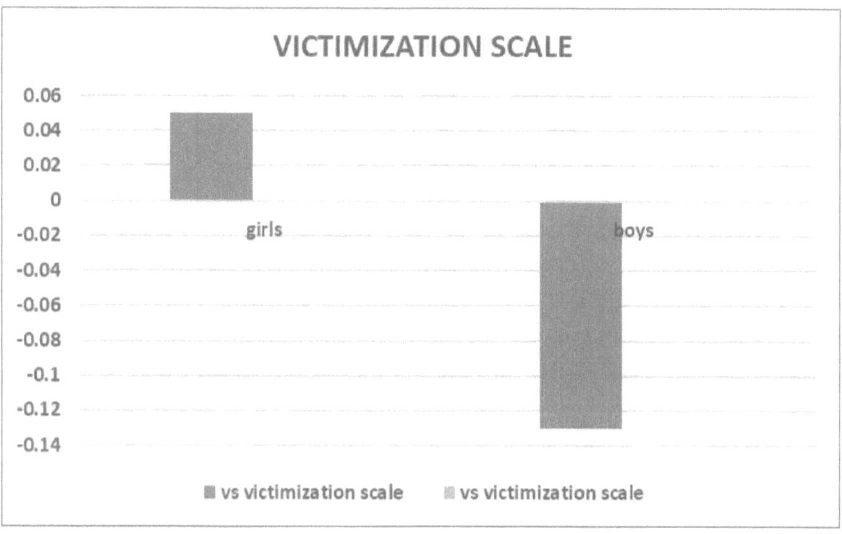

The survey showed that girls perceive the environment as more threatening than boys. According to the results, unlike boys, girls display more such physical, psychological, or social signs that increase their likelihood of becoming victims. However, this may be conditioned by our cultural peculiarities; boys usually find talking about emotions much more difficult than girls do. Patriarchal culture, or masculism, requires boys to be more reserved; hence, while taking the test, girls may be more honest than boys. This factor may have caused the difference in the results.

While analyzing the results from a gender perspective, it becomes even more interesting that during the literature review for our thesis, girls tend to protest violence and oppression more than boys (Salmivalli, 2001). They appear to be more sensitive to the aggressive environment, and perhaps because of that, we obtained the result in our study that girls tend to perceive the environment as more threatening than boys do.

Analysis of the differences between means of the types of school culture and victimization indicators by regions showed statistically significant results (see table 23). Particularly, we identified the differences between regions by school culture types of "isolation," "wellness," and "threat" also by the mean of the victimization scale: $F\,(5) = 2.389$, $p = 0.008$; $F\,(5) = 3.429$, $p = 0.000$; $F\,(5) = 13.275$, $p = 0.000$; $F\,(4) = 22.073$, $p = 0.000$, respectively.

Mean						
q0170 I live	sk_g isolation	sk_k wellness	sk_s threat	sk_t equality	bd aggression	vs victimization scale
Tbilisi	0.02	-0.08	0.20	-0.01	0.01	0.02
Imereti	0.61	-0.41	1.45	-0.95	0.57	0.29
Mtskheta-Mtianeti	-0.29	0.42	-0.49	0.28	-0.08	-0.25

Kvemo Kartli	-0.58	0.36	-0.33	-1.61	0.62	-0.01
Shida Kartli	-0.13	0.27	-0.30	0.10	-0.16	-0.22
Other regions	0.87	-0.29	0.88	-0.79	0.32	3.57
sig	*0.008*	*0.000*	*0.000*	0.065	*0.074*	*0.000*

Let us review each of them separately. The school culture type "isolation" is highest in the group "other regions" (0.87), as well as in Imereti region (0.61). The mean of "isolation" is the lowest among the regions in Kvemo Kartli (–.58). According to this parameter, we have mean indicator in Tbilisi (0.02) and below mean in Mtskheta-Mtianeti and Shida Kartli (–0.29 and –.0.13, respectively).

The mean indicator of wellness-type school culture is highest in Mtskheta-Mtaineti region (0.42), followed by Kvemo Kartli (0.36) and Shida Kartli (0.27). In Tbilisi, the wellness indicator is slightly below mean (–0.08), while in Imereti, mean wellness indicators of school culture is very low (–0.41). This figure is relatively low also in "other regions" (–0.29).

School culture type "threat" is rather high in Imereti (1.45) and "in other regions" (0.88). This indicator is significantly lower than mean in Mskheta-Mtianeti (–0.49), Kvemo Kartli (–0.33), and Shida Kartli (–0.30).

The mean indicator of the school culture type "threat" in Tbilisi is rather high (0.20).

In regard to the victimization scale, it is especially high in "other regions" (3.57), followed by Imereti region, where this indicator is also rather high (0.29). In Tbilisi and Kvemo Kartli, the indicator of victimization is at the average level (0.02 and –0.01, respectively), and in Mtskheta-Mtianeti and Shida Kartli, the victimization indicator is rather low (0.25 and −0.22, respectively).

The difference between the different types of school culture and means of victimization indicators by region is presented in graphics 13–16.

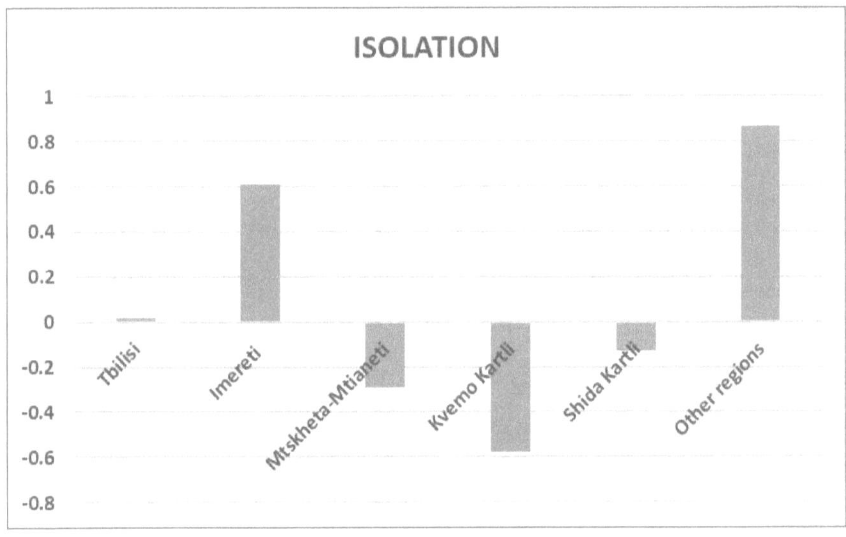

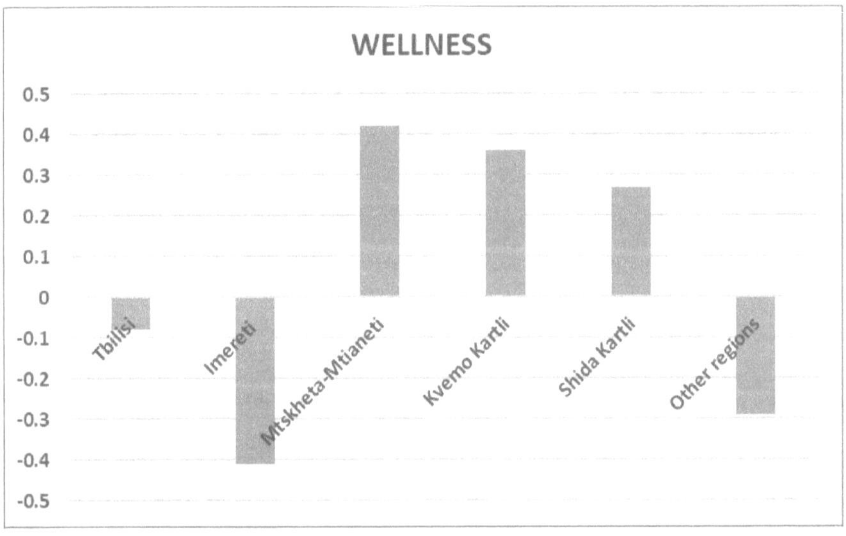

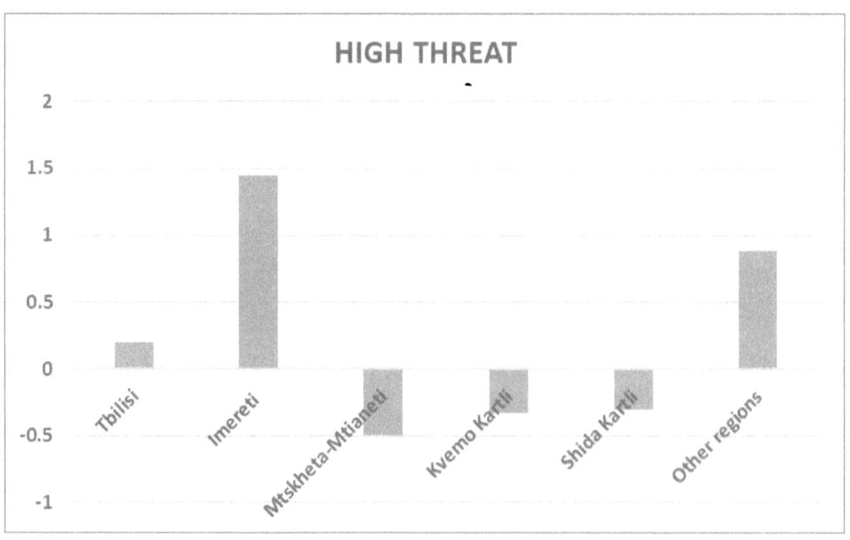

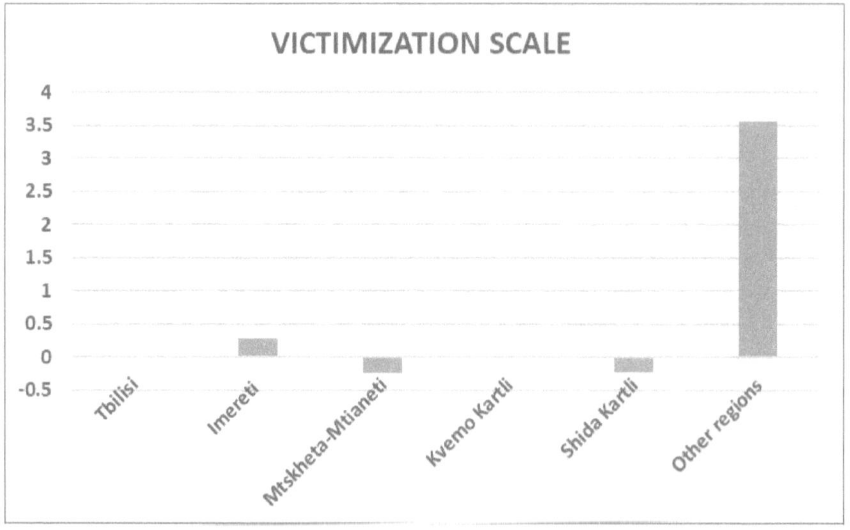

As shown above, while considering the regression model, some values of the variables—region, age, parental employment—are predictors of victimization. However, the comparison of the means of the results by these variables gives a different picture. This is especially true for age and region variables (diagrams N and N). In this context, we consider it important to analyze the obtained different pictures of victimization and school culture means in the context of these variables. The point is that the regression model considers the influence of regions on victimization independently of other parameters involved in the regression. And when comparing the means, we also have the impact of other variables. So, for example, let us consider the example of regions when comparing the means by regions. Regions differ from each other by other variables participating in the regression, and this difference gives us a different picture. In the evaluation of the quality of victimization, when we look at the regression model, the share of the region is 4.5 percent, and the rest of the variables 95.5 percent. So when comparing the means by regions, we are not protected from the influence of parameters that differentiate the regions.

3

SUMMARY AND DISCUSSION

The hierarchical regression model constructed by us was able to explain 34 percent of the victimization; 73 percent is conditioned by the combination of variables of the educational environment and aggression. Particularly, we assumed that despite the aggression level, the safe school environment significantly reduces the cases of bullying. More precisely, we can state that independent of the aggression level, the safe school environment conditions a low victimization level, and despite the aggression level, the unsafe school environment conditions a high victimization level.

As it was previously demonstrated, despite the aggression level, the safe school environment reduces victimization level. The school environment "benevolence," even in combination with aggression, is a negative predictor of victimization. The school environment "equality" is also a negative predictor. However, at the background of aggression, it loses its statistical significance that refers to the fact that "equality" in comparison to "benevolence" is a variable with a lesser impact.

The regression model proved that despite the aggression level, the unsafe school environment conditions a high victimization indicator. The survey demonstrated that two variables of the school environment—"threat" and "isolation"—in combination with aggression represent strong positive predictors.

Thus, the survey proved that bullying occurs if there is presence of aggression, presence of a potential victim, and a favorable environment for the realization of this behavior. Consequently, we can conclude that despite the aggression level, the safe school environment significantly reduces the cases of bullying, and the unsafe school environment conditions a high victimization indicator.

Concurrently, we assumed that cases of bullying would occur among boys more often than among girls, in big schools rather than in smaller ones, and among those children whose neither parents are employed. In the case of the first two hypotheses, the survey did not give us statistically reliable data. Hence, the given hypotheses were not proved.

It should be noted, however, that the survey revealed the connection of bullying with parental employment. It turned out that parental unemployment is a predictor of victimization. Particularly, it showed that when neither of the parents of a teenager are employed, he or she is more prone to victimization.

The student variables "age" and "residential region"—Shida Kartli and so-called other regions—also demonstrated statistically significant predictive values. It turned out that bullying is more anticipated among fifteen-year-old students and in the previously mentioned regions. Despite the fact that predictive value of the variables of certain regions is statistically significant, this issue, in our opinion, requires additional research since, as a result of in-depth research, the analysis of this variable can reveal predominant predictive weight of some of its components.

We can generalize the results and conclude, that:

- Bullying behavior occurs when there is a victim, and the environment allows the realization of aggression.
- School culture is a strong predictor of bullying behavior.
- The probability of becoming a victim (victimhood) is high among those teenagers who experience high levels of stress in the environment.
- When a teenager experiences a sense of threat, he or she develops physical, psychological, or social symptoms that make him or her vulnerable to bullying.
- Schools should display such an environment where the set, preconditioning bullying behavior is not enhanced.
- A school culture should be fostered that is oriented to adherence to the rules of communication and mutual respect in the group as it reduces the likelihood of a teenager becoming a victim. Consequently, when a teenager has a sense of wellness even in combination with aggression, this sense reduces the likelihood of a teenager to become a victim.

The likelihood of turning into a victim is high among those teenagers who experience a sense of high threat in the school environment, while a school culture that is oriented to adherence to communications rules and mutual respect (that is, a teenager experiences wellness) reduces the probability of teenagers becoming victims.

The review of recent literature showed that many theories try to explain bullying behavior, but most of the theories highlight the reasons for the realization of a social act, where attempts to explain the psychological model of bullying are very few. Such approaches as social learning, development, resilience, dominance, ecological systems, organizational culture, and other theories mostly focus their attention on this-or-that aspect and offer answers to the question, What is characteristic for bullying, and how it is realized? In the case of our work, we decided to conduct an in-depth study of this issue with the goal of determining how the psychological mechanism of bullying works and studying the bullying behavior at the level of an individual. Therefore, we analyzed this complex and multicomponent behavior based on the theory of set.

The survey showed that the theory of set perfectly explains the emergence of the set required for the realization and mechanism of bullying at the individual level. Particularly, it allows us not only to explain current behaviors and situations but to predict the emergence or disappearance of a behavior by means of managing instrumental conditions. The theory of set shows us how to get the bully out of the practice of being engaged in this aggressive behavior by suppressing the set. It also teaches us how to prevent such behavior.

The survey revealed that safe school culture is a type of instrumental condition that does not allow the set underlying the aggressive behavior to be realized.

Most likely at this time, the relevant fixed set acquires the form of an unrealized set and is being maintained in this way. However, when the environment is systematically safe, this reality should lead us to the breakdown of the fixed set underlying bullying that facilitates extinguishing of the current set and development of a new adequate set.

The theory of set enables us to realize this process takes a long time. When the set for its realization does not provide instrumental conditions, it is not enough for this set to be extinguished and replaced by a new one. Its transformation requires time. It is important that the old set does not have the chance to be realized on a regular basis. According to the theory, as soon as there is a favorable environment for the old set to be realized, relevant behavior will immediately occur that will again facilitate enhancement of the old set. Hence, it should be explained to school administrators and teachers at the recommendation level that the extinguishing of the set underlying the aggressive behavior or the process of its replacement is the result of consistent and long-term work. They should not expect improvement overnight.

In addition, when we are dealing with an unrealized set, there is always a threat that in one environment (class, school), the set that moved into unrealized condition could still be striving toward realization in a more favorable environment. It is important not to create a favorable environment for the realization of bullying behavior and fixation of the underlying set. Rather, create a favorable environment for the realization of sets that had moved into an unrealized condition. Consequently, for both extinguishing the fixed set and allowing the emergence of the new one, consistent and persistent work is required. Understanding the mechanism of the set that triggers emergence and realization of bullying shows the difficulties of its extinguishing, which in its turn makes it clear why bullying behavior is so difficult to manage and why its spreading has such a large-scale character.

The construct of bullying behavior is well explained by a set mechanism, the action and self-development theory, which offers us a complete picture of bullying. This theory explains the reason a particular teenager becomes a bully, the psychological mechanism that underlies the formation of a bully, how bullying behavior can be revealed, and the conditions that facilitate its emergence.

To summarize, our survey uncovered an interesting picture for educational psychology. The survey findings are interesting for school education and policy planning. It should be noted that in addition to the study of psychological predictors, our survey provides information about school culture, aggression, and victimization with the parameters of gender, region, age, and others. We believe our findings will also assist in preventing bullying behaviors in the education system.

The survey conducted in terms of the dissertation also outlined new topics for further exploration. We believe that it will be interesting to further study the connections between the types of environment and aggression level; correlations between school climate, aggression levels, and the forms of victimization; how common an aggressive behavior is for the victim himself or herself, and so on. It will also be interesting to explore the relationships between background and personal aggression. Since we know that bullying is a social behavior, it always has its "attending audience," it would be wrong to perceive it as a behavior occurring only on a personal level. Hence, we believe that additional study of the background aggression will be interesting.

LIMITATIONS OF THE SURVEY

1. Prior to starting the fieldwork, we intended to apply quota sampling for the population under exploration. Particularly, together with the Ministry of Education, Science, Culture and Sports, we selected particular schools whose students we intended to interview. However, due to the pandemic caused by the new coronavirus and accompanying restrictions, we were unable to observe the principle of quota sampling. Because of that, we applied the available sampling method, though we realized that decision bore certain risks. The survey identified regional variables "Shida Kartli" and so-called other regions as one of the predictors of bullying. It is obvious that quota sampling would have given us a much more precise picture in that regard.

Despite this fact, it should be noted that our goal was to study the psychological mechanism of bullying and to construct a relevant regression model, not a reliable and representative description of bullying in the country or region. We have obtained a large and diverse amount of data in terms of the variables important for the survey, which enables us to conduct an interesting statistical analysis.

2. We applied three questionnaires as a statistical instrument with more than one hundred provisions. Filling out the questionnaires required a lot of time from teenagers, which might have affected our findings.

Despite the limitations, we believe the survey provided us with valuable findings that have both theoretical and practical importance. The survey conducted will facilitate understanding of the theoretical construct of bullying and contribute to the study of the psychological nature of bullying. We believe the recommendations based on the survey will also facilitate general education policy planning in Georgia.

REFERENCES

Bagwell, C., & Schmidt, M. (2011). *Friendships in Childhood and Adolescence.* The Guilford Press.

Bandura, A. (1973). *Aggression: A Social Learning Analysis.*

Bandura, A. (1978). Social learning theory. *Journal of Communication.*

Bandura, A. (1983). Psychological mechanisms of aggression. *Aggression: Theoretical and empirical reviews.*

Bauman, S. (2011). *Cyberbullying: What Counselors Need to Know.* American Counseling Association.

Berkowitz, L., & Knurek, D. A. (1969). Label-mediated hostility generalization. *Journal of Personality and Social Psychology, 13*(3), 200–206. https://doi.org/10.1037/h0028125

Bowman, D. (2018). *The Sociology of Bullying: Prevention and Intervention Using a Three Themed Model.*

Brighton, H., & Sayeed, L. (1990). The pervasiveness of senior management's view of the cultural gaps within a division. *Groups and Organization Studies,* 266–278.

Bronfenbrenner, U. (1979). *The Ecology of Human Development: Experiments by Nature and Design.* Harvard University Press.

Craig, G. J. (2001). *Human Development.* Upper Saddle River, N.J.: Prentice Hall.

Gaffney, H., Farrington, D. P., & Ttofi, M. M. (2019). Examining the effectiveness of school-bullying intervention programs globally. *International Journal of Bullying Prevention.*

Gegehr, C. (2001). Cognitive-behavioral theory. In N. P. Lehmann, *Theoretical Perspectives for Direct Social Work Practice, a Generalist-Eclectic Approach* (pp. 165–182). New York: Springer Publishing.

Kaukiainen, C. S. (1996). *Bullying as a group process: Participant roles and their relations to social status within the group.* Retrieved from Wiley Online Library.

Klein, J., Cornell, D., & Konold, T. (2012). Relationship between bullying, school climate, and student risk behaviors. *School Psychology Quarterly.*

Kubiszewski, V. F. (2015). Does cyberbullying overlap with school bullying when taking modality of involvement into account. *Computers in Human Behaviour,* 49–57.

Lee, C. (2004). *Preventing Bullying in Schools: A guide for Teachers and Other Professionals.* London: Paul Chapman Publishing.

Lee, C., & Song, J. (2012). Functions of parental involvement and effects of school climate on bullying behaviors among South Korean middle school students. *Journal of Interpersonal Violence.*

Li, Q. (2010). Cyberbullying in high schools: A study of student's behaviors and beliefs about this new phenomenon. *Journal of Agression, Maltreatment & Trauma,* 372–391.

Milner, R. (2020). *Start Where You Are, But Don't Stay There.*

Olweus, D. (1993). *Bullying at School: What We Know and What We Can Do.* Blackwell.

Salmivalli, C. (2001). *Group View on Victimization: Empirical Findings and Their Implications.* New York: Guilford Press.

Swearer, S. (2015). Understanding the psychology of bullying. *American Psychologist*, 344-350.

Unnever, J. D. (2004). Middle school victims of bullying: Who reports being bullied? *Aggressive Behavior*, 373–388

ნადირაშვილი, შ. (2001). განწყობის ანტროპული თეორია. თბილისი: საქართველოს მეცნიერებათა აკადემიის დ. უზნაძის სახელობის ფსიქოლოგიის ინსტიტუტი.

უზნაძე,დ. (1977). განწყობის ფსიქოლოგიის ექსპერიმენტული საფუძვლები - ტომი *VI*. მეცნიერება.

უზნაძე, დ. (1977). ტომი *VI*. თბილისი: მეცნიერება.

www.ingramcontent.com/pod-product-compliance
Lightning Source LLC
Chambersburg PA
CBHW051412250726
48655CB00003B/1011